TEACHING ENGLISH ONLINE

Leyla N. M. Norman

Table of Contents

Introduction

Google "online ESL jobs" or something similar and you'll be inundated with opportunities to work from home as an English as a second language teacher. Students around the world want to learn English. It is essential for their futures. The only way many people have access to a native speaker is online.

I have taught ESL in U.S. public charter schools, in adult learning centers, in an academic language school that prepares students for university in the U.S., in a private school to one student, in housewives' homes, in libraries. I also have taught and continue to teach ESL online. I am by far not the most experienced or knowledgeable ESL teacher out there. I am not formally educated in computers.

What I am passionate about, though, are my students, their lives, their pasts, their hopes for the future. Some of them I get to work with in person, and there are some who I have taught online. I have worked for a few ESL tutoring companies, and I have worked for myself. Using interactive whiteboards, my phone, and Skype, I have been able to teach English and share life with some amazing individuals around the U.S. and around the world. I have myself been an online Spanish student with a great teacher from Guatemala.

Technology can be a royal pain in the backside. I know that well. I have had to cancel lessons, turn off my video, restart my computer two minutes before a lesson was to start with no way to contact students, and the list goes on. However, its potential in online language learning is phenomenal.

In 2014, I left my job working in a public school and took my very part-time ESL tutoring company, Empower English Tutoring (http://www.empowerenglishtutoring.com) to the next level. I am still a very modest, one-woman show, but I have stayed busy enough to help pay my family's bills.

As of early 2015, about half of my students are online. I am constantly changing how I teach them to try to keep them engaged and learning. What you will read about concerns some of my experiences and ways I was trained or discovered on my own to solve them. This book includes some activity ideas to help you create your own online lessons as well.

The interactive whiteboard is a powerful tool to use in online teaching. It goes beyond instant messaging in Skype. My hope is that you pick up a few tips to help your lessons go more smoothly and that you find your own ways to engage your students and just have fun teaching using some of these ideas as a springboard.

Intended Audience

This book's purpose is not to convince you to become a full-time (Full-time hours are rare anyway in teaching online.) online ESL teacher, nor is it to give you tips on how to start your own online ESL tutoring business. I wrote it with ESL teachers who already work online in mind and for ESL teachers who may already want to begin teaching online. They may work for already-established ESL tutoring companies, or they may work for themselves.

Purpose of the Book

I've sat through a few online ESL tutoring companies' training programs, and I've learned a lot of things about teaching online the hard way. My goal is for you to improve your delivery of online ESL lessons.

When you improve your overall technique, you get better student feedback, which as you probably know, some ESL tutoring companies use in their assessments of how much to pay you. I worked for one company that encouraged students to rate me each lesson in a number of domains. I received a base pay, but if students rated me high, I got a "bonus," which significantly increased my hourly rate. Likewise, if you have your own business, and you have online students happy with your work, they may be willing to write honest testimonials for your website or refer you to their colleagues or friends.

The way to get better feedback from students is to engage them, make the lesson fun and relevant, and get their minds ready to learn from the moment you and your students log in to the online classroom. When students are mentally prepared to learn and stay interested throughout the lesson, they are likely to retain more of what you teach them.

1

Features of Online Whiteboards

The greatest feature of tangible or virtual whiteboards, in my opinion, is that they are in no way associated with the fingernail-on-the chalkboard sound from my childhood. Beyond this, however, online whiteboards offer opportunities to interact with your students in ways that are difficult to in an in-person environment.

First, you and your students can all be in the same online classroom at the same time. Depending on the particular whiteboard you use, you can have two students or dozens in the class simultaneously. This works great if you have large classes of ESL students. Most teachers, however, will find that teaching more than about four ESL students at one time in an online environment is not beneficial to them or to the students. When you research which whiteboard or particular plan a whiteboard provider offers, think about how many students you have and how many students will be in the same class at one time. For me, it has always made sense to have low numbers of users in the room at the same time, but to pay extra for a few classrooms. ESL teachers are typically not running webinars to massive numbers of students, so having a few students per class is probably the way to go. However, if you branch out a little and join one of the many online tutoring hosting sites that allow you to create large, self-guided courses for students, say, on how to improve your pronunciation, you can build some extra income on these sites.

The reason I liked to have extra classrooms is that I can save chats, screens, and slides with individual students from class to class. Each classroom is password-protected, so I can be sure that only the students and I have access to it between classes. I use a program called Scribblar that I can connect to right from my website. Currently this program does not offer a lot of other features I like, such as shared web browsing, share screen, or video conferencing (although you can open Skype from within the program), but the ability to save material from class to class is more important to me than these. I use Skype for the other capabilities. This enables students to take notes from the whiteboard later, take screenshots for future reference, or to perhaps complete some homework I assigned. Note that not all whiteboard programs or online tutoring hosting sites offer this capability.

Many of them require you to schedule a class, and once the class has ended, all of the material you used to teach and your students' work is gone. This kind of program is not optimal, in my opinion, although it does serve the basic purpose of facilitating online ESL teaching.

The ability to upload documents and images is integral to an online whiteboard. You can upload worksheets, documents you create with explanations, quizzes, PowerPoint presentations, PDF documents, etc. These all allow you to give your students visuals to enhance their understanding and the opportunity to practice what you teach, say, in a fill-in-the-blank exercise.

Uploading images is a good way to provide a definition of a word, or to spur a conversation. Pictures in your PowerPoints or in vocabulary matching exercises are just a couple of ways to use images in the online classroom.

Online whiteboards also allow you to video and audio conference with your students. Many of them have these two features (or at least audio) built in. When you can see your students in a video chat, you can better tell whether or not they understand what you have said based on facial expression. It also allows you more freedom to share and understand humor during lessons by showing a smiling or laughing face. Audio conferencing enables your students to talk to you and to ask questions. If you are the only moderator in the classroom, you can have your students raise their hands to ask a question in a large class, and give each student his individual turn to speak by turning his microphone on or off in the class. Students can also use the chat box to communicate with you.

Additionally, a few whiteboard programs let you conduct shared web browsing sessions with your class. So in the classroom, your students will all be able to see the article on the website you want them to read, or maybe you look up words in an online dictionary and want students to decide on the correct definition of a multiple-meaning word. You can share screens in Skype as well, and this is free for calls between two people. However, if you can do this in the classroom and share it with more than one person (without extra fees for group calls like in Skype), it streamlines the technological aspect of learning online and decreases student – and your – frustration. Note that some versions of Skype may not support sharing screens.

The text writer feature of online whiteboards is a tool that you can use to increase interaction in the online classroom with your students. For example, you can have them write a paragraph, edit each other's writing, or write down your or another student's dictation. Text can be written in different colors, in bold or italics, and in several fonts. These options enable all classroom participants to share their ideas and draw attention to particular words or sentences. The typical online whiteboard also offers a highlighter and pointer. You could use this to emphasize a particular area of your student's writing that needs attention. Using the highlighter, you can perhaps change colors for different kinds of errors. Use green for grammar errors and blue for spelling mistakes. Your student can then correct herself.

For when you feel like playing Pictionary with your students or drawing a definition of a word, you can use the shape tool in an online classroom. Draw different colored circles (filled or unfilled with your favorite color) with varying line thicknesses to create a snowman to illustrate that word. Draw a box around a particular area of a worksheet you uploaded a student forgot to do. The shape tool is not limited to just a few uses. Its possibilities are like those of the text and highlighter tool: whatever you can imagine, you can probably do with it to help your students improve their English.

The drawing tool allows you to freehand draw or write in different line thicknesses and colors. You have more flexibility with this tool to create what you want on the whiteboard screen, but note that it is not very neat for underlining or writing. Minimize its usage to perhaps drawing a picture or drawing an arrow to an important area of the screen.

While not nearly as inspiring as colored text or shapes, you have to admit that erasing objects and pages is a very useful aspect of online whiteboards. When you make a mistake, you can instantly erase it. Students can use the tools as well. When you have finished a lesson, you can erase an entire page and use it for the next one.

Finally, the chat box is an extra feature of most whiteboards that enable you to talk with your students. If you cannot understand something your students say, ask them to write it in the chat box (or on the whiteboard). If you are having audio problems, explain the situation in the chat box. Send your students links to outside websites if you don't have shared browsing. Chatting is also a great way to greet your students as you wait for them to all arrive for class.

2

Problem Areas for Teachers and Students

Do you remember a class in school or college that you dreaded going to because it was boring? One of mine was college geology. I loved the subject, but, man, the instructor was awful. I was a jerk in class and talked a lot. This was significant because I had never before gotten in trouble for anything in school—except maybe reading books in class. The instructor actually kicked my two collaborators and me out into the hall when he'd finally had enough.

As an online instructor, you are going to have to face an even more distractable audience. Students could just as easily be checking the scores of their favorite teams or maybe watching their favorite movie in the background on Netflix.

To ensure that your lessons are interesting, keep two considerations in mind. First, lay out the lesson objectives and structure for your students at the beginning of class. Additionally, change the type of activities in the lesson regularly.

Pacing

Having your students read one text for the entire sixty minutes of your lesson can be incredibly monotonous. To keep your students engaged, however, by working with the same text but changing the activities you do during the lesson every ten to fifteen minutes, your students are better able to concentrate on the content of the lesson.

For example, if you ask your students a background question about the topic of the text to get them thinking about the text's subject before they read, you practice conversation, speaking, and listening. You also have the chance at this point to bring up new vocabulary words the students will encounter in the text and to discuss their meanings. This might take about five minutes.

Then have your students skim the article, noting any headlines, captions, bolded words, etc. Have the students-report on the article's contents. Tell the students to make predictions about what the article may be about. This may take about five minutes. Then read the article out loud to the students and have them highlight unknown words. Discuss the vocabulary. The students can then read the article aloud, and you work on pronunciation next. This might take fifteen minutes.

Next, you might work on reading comprehension with verbal or written questions the students work on. This can take fifteen minutes. Spend time having your students work on mastering vocabulary, writing a summary or answer to a critical thinkking question about the article, or perhaps reading fluency. This might take the remaining twenty minutes of class.

While this is a very rough outline of what you could do during class, the main point is that you want to keep your students paying attention by changing up activities during the lesson regularly.

Lesson Outline

Introduce the lesson objective(s) to your students from the beginning of class. Let them know what activities they will be doing during class. For example, you might say at the beginning of the lesson on the article mentioned previously, "Today, we will take a look at a business article about writing business emails. By the end of the lesson you will be able to use five new vocabulary words from the article, and answer questions about the article in complete sentences using the simple present tense in speaking and in writing."

The reason for presenting an outline – a useful strategy in both traditional and online classrooms – is to get your students thinking about what they will learn. They know what to expect and are more mentally ready to participate in the lesson.

Student Interaction

Many students encounter boredom in an online classroom when they are not actively engaged in the lesson. This means that all they are doing is listening. If they are not getting the chance to speak, write on the whiteboard, draw, or talk to other students, they quickly become disenchanted with online ESL classes.

Your goal should be to have your students speak about eighty percent of the time in class. This means that you ask guiding questions and let them do the rest. Get them to write on the whiteboard and find each other's mistakes in speaking and writing. Students often complain that they do not get as much practice as they want in group classes, so make sure that you allow enough time for each student to practice all four areas of learning a language: listening, speaking, reading, and writing.

3

Technical Considerations to Improve Teaching

Using Audio Conferencing

Audio conferencing allows you to communicate by voice with your student. Many online whiteboard programs offer audio conferencing features. Free online whiteboards usually do not have an audio conferencing feature, so many teachers have to use another VOiP provider, such as Google Hangouts or Skype. These free services offer video conferencing as well.

Audio problems can completely ruin a lesson, and they can cause embarrassment in a lesson, too. For example, I have had more than one lesson in which the lag between my voice and my student caused me to give the student the answer to a question I asked because I thought he or she needed help. I have also ended up talking over my student, which just lead to lots of confusion and apologies. This is wasted time that could have been spent actually learning.

Types of Problems with Audio Conferencing

1. Lag Time

You and your students will likely experience lag time at some point during your online classes. This occurs when you or your student says something, but one of you doesn't hear it until a second or two later.

2. *Echo, Echo, Echo*

Echo problems occur when you or your student uses the external speakers on their computers instead of a headset to hear what the other is saying. You or your students hear themselves speaking, and it is really distracting and very difficult to speak over.

3. *Microphone*

Sometimes it can be difficult to hear your students or for your students to hear you if one of you uses the microphone integrated into your laptop, tablet, or smartphone. You waste time asking each other to repeat yourselves. Each moment in your lesson is precious, so make sure you can actually hear your students and that they can hear you.

Solutions for Audio Problems

When audio problems occur, you have a few options to solve them. It's best, however, to try to prevent problems before a lesson. Let's take a look at ways to prevent problems first.

Prevention

1. *Have More Than One Way to Contact Your Students*

Get your students' phone numbers so that you have a back-up way to contact them if online audio conferencing fails. You can also use your smartphone to call your students on Skype or some other online audio conferencing program.

Consider investing in an extra tablet or computer that allows you to use Skype or that allows you to contact your students if one device fails. If your computer's battery dies, or it suddenly needs to restart after downloading updates (This has happened to me.), it is vital that you have another way to talk to your students, even if it is just to send a text message or IM.

Sign up on more than one audio conferencing platform, and have your students do the same. Skype, Google Hangouts, Yahoo Messenger, QQ (popular in China) are just a few that you can use.

2. Wired Internet

It is vital that you have access to high speed Internet if you teach online. It is also important to have a wired ethernet connection as well. This is important for video conferencing, especially. If you have wireless in your home or office, and it works for your lessons, that is fine. However, if you find that you have audio problems, consider turning off your wifi and then hardwiring your computer to the Internet through an ethernet connection. Your connection may improve.

Another consideration: if you use wireless in the room in which you work, but you don't have ethernet access there, ensure that you have immediate access to the room with ethernet and that it is an appropriate place to work.

3. Get a Good Headset

Echo problems and not being able to hear your students can often be prevented if you AND your students have good-quality headsets with a microphone. Be sure that the headphones and microphone are compatible with your computer. Newer computers often have one outlet that is for audio and video instead of the older, pink and green audio and video jacks.

4. Pre-Lesson Check

About fifteen minutes before your lesson is to start, turn on your computer, log in to your online white-board program, sign in to Skype, Hangouts, etc., and be sure that all of your equipment is working properly. This gives you time to restart your computer if you need to and to contact your students if you have to solve a technical problem to mention you may be a few minutes late.

Solving Audio Problems During the Lesson

Even if you have taken all of the steps listed above to prevent audio problems, sometimes problems with listening and speaking to your students will occur. Here are some ways to try to solve the audio problems without losing too much time in the lesson or having to cancel it.

1. Double Check Connections

Make sure your headset's volume is turned up, and that volume is turned up on your computer. Ensure that your ethernet or wireless is functioning properly. Check that your computer's volume is up. If you have an older computer with separate jacks for audio and video, be sure your headset's audio jack is plugged in all the way and that you don't accidentally have the video jack plugged in to the audio jack.

2. Contact Your Students via a Different Medium

Call your students on the phone. Use your tablet to place a Skype call. Use the chatbox in the online whiteboard program to tell your students you're having technical problems and what you are trying to do to solve the problem. Send an IM in Skype, or via another messenger.

3. Hang Up and Try Again

If you need to, hang up the call, and try to contact your students again. You may need to use a different audio program for this, or maybe the phone. You may also need to reboot your computer.

4. Turn Off Video

If you are using video, turn it off. This can improve audio performance.

Make sure your students check these possibilities as well.

Watching a Video Online

If you use a shared browsing feature in your online whiteboard program or you send your student to an outside website to watch a short video (i.e., a pronunciation video on YouTube), your students may have technical problems with the audio and/or the video. If this occurs, you could try sharing your screen in Skype or a similar program and turning your video up all the way so your students can hear it.

Using Video Conferencing

Video conferencing is a vital component of an online whiteboard program. If your program does not offer it, I would encourage you to use Skype, Google Hangouts, or a similar program if you can. You may have to pay extra for group calls if you have more than one student in a lesson, but the subscription would be worth the benefits you and your students receive.

One of the benefits of video conferencing when teaching ESL online is that you can see if your students are confused, can't hear you, or have other difficulties. You can also more easily share humor and see how your students are feeling in general during a class.

When video problems occur, it is possible to continue the lesson with audio only. However, it is always best to try to prevent and solve video problems if you can.

Prevention of Video Problems

1. Think Ethernet

As mentioned previously, having wired, high speed internet is ideal for teaching ESL online. Video usually does not perform as well with wifi connections. In fact, in my experience, many online ESL tutoring companies will not hire teachers who only have wifi. The decline in overall lesson quality is such that they don't even consider hiring qualified teachers without an ethernet connection.

2. Check Your Camera

When you do your audio check, also be sure that your camera is working properly. You can do this by opening your computer's camera program or app and seeing if you can see yourself. Skype also offers video and audio checks to be sure the other person or people can see/hear you well.

Troubleshooting Video Problems

If you encounter video problems during your lessons, here are some steps you can take to try to solve them.

1. Turn Off Your Web Cam

Encourage your students to turn their camera off when you do. This can help improve the overall quality of the call.

2. End the Call

Call your student back, and try to turn on the camera again. You might also need to restart your computer. Additionally, just as with audio conferencing, it is important for you to have other options to contact your students. If you experience video problems, you may need to use another platform from which to contact your students via video. You may also need another device, such as a back-up computer, a tablet, or a smartphone.

Note that if you use a tablet or other mobile device, make sure that you can actually use the device to log into the online whiteboard program if you use it for your video conferencing. This is something to check before your lesson ever starts. You may be able to continue using the online whiteboard program for written interaction, but you might need to use Skype, Google Hangouts, or another device with one of these programs to continue using video with your students.

How to Handle a Total Technological Failure

If the technical problems go on for more than ten minutes, it is probably best to tell the student that you will refund the cost of the lesson or reschedule at a convenient time for him. Consider offering a partial refund instead of a full refund if the lesson was able to continue successfully for fifteen or more minutes. You could also add the number of missed minutes onto the next lesson if it is convenient for you and your students.

There is no point fighting technology if it is simply not going to work. Apologize, and try again at a later time.

4

Share Screen

Sharing your screen with your students, or vice versa, is another important collaborative tool when you teach ESL online. There are several free share screen programs you can use online, which may include an audio conferencing feature. Note that if you use these free programs, you limit your students' interaction with the lesson, and you risk having too many accounts links to send to your students. Too many tools may create confusion for you and your students. Paying a subscription fee to a web conferencing program makes more sense in the long run and simplifies your teaching.

Some Ways to Use Share Screen

I am a fan of Moby Max. This is an online program that provides my students with a placement test for grammar and vocabulary (among many other amazing features), and then it gives them self-guided lessons in areas in which they need to improve. I like to see my students work through Moby Max for about ten to fifteen minutes per lesson. For this, I use share screen in Skype. My current web conferencing program (Scribblar) does not feature video conferencing, so I use Skype for that, audio, and for sharing screens with my students.

You might also use share screen as a last resort to share a document with your student. If you can't get Google

Drive or Docs to work, you can't upload to your online whiteboard, and you want your students to see exactly what you're talking about on a document, share screen may be another way to do so. For example, if you want your student to identify a grammar mistake in her writing, you can highlight the line in Word, and then share the screen quickly with the student. This saves time over emailing the document or trying to send it through an instant messenger, which sometimes does not quite work the way it should.

Additionally, your students may have a hard time watching a particular video you want them to see. You can share it via share screen and turn up the volume on your speakers (after unplugging your headphones, of course). This is definitely not ideal, but if the video is really important to your lesson, it is likely better than not seeing it at all.

Another way to use share screen is to play online ESL games or take grammar or vocabulary quizzes. Your students can share their screens with you, and you can watch and guide them they work through the exercises. You can also share your screen with your students and have them tell you which answer they want to choose if they are unable to get the game, quiz, or exercise to load and function properly on their computers. These types of activities are good for end-of-lesson reviews or as a warm-up. They create a lighter mood in the class and help your students to focus on the lesson.

Furthermore, share screen is good for sharing an online article with your students. If your students cannot get their computers to load a particular article that you want to read with them, share screen is another option to share it. Remember, this should be used as a last resort. If possible, simply copy and paste the article with the hyperlink to it into a document that you save to your computer, and then upload into the online whiteboard. You might also take a screen shot of it. If you do the screen shot, know that you may have to scroll up and down or over to see the entire image.

Finally, share screen is a good, quick way to share an image online that illustrates a word's definition. Rather than sending your student a link through the chat box in the web conferencing program or through instant messenger, you can just share screens quickly to demonstrate the meaning of a new vocabulary word. Another way to do this is also to do shared web browsing with your students if your web conferencing program offers it or to save the image to your computer and then upload it to the whiteboard.

A Word of Caution with Share Screen

Make sure you close any tabs or documents that you don't want your students to see before you initiate the share screen feature. This can result in some embarrassing situations. Also, be sure you turn off share screen when it is time to. If you happen to check your email (Let's hope your attention is focused on the lesson, but I have to admit I have done this.), you really want to make sure that your share screen is turned off.

When you are looking at the same screen as your students, it increases the overall interaction of the lesson. It makes it more fun, and it can also serve as a last resort if you have technical difficulties in sharing documents or multimedia resources with your students.

5

Interactive Activities for Online ESL Teaching

Your imagination is really the limit for what kinds of activities you can use in your online ESL classroom. The more interactive they are, and the more you vary the activities within a lesson and between the lessons, the more you and your students will like a class.

Fill in the Blank

Fill in the blank exercises get students writing and encourage them to get involved in class. They are perfect for all levels of ESL students (provided, of course, that you're not teaching very young children, which is definitely possible online – I have taught a three year-old, and we spent most of our time singing).

Plenty of online fill-in-the-blank activities are available for free online, and you can definitely create your own based on a text that you and your student read together, or perhaps based on a short video clip you watch.

For lower-level students and for the first couple of times that your students encounter a new vocabulary word, use word banks. Word banks help your students to identify the answer, while if you don't provide a word bank, your students have to remember the word without any prompts. This latter activity requires more in-depth, critical thinking than just identifying the word from a short list. Word banks also enocurage your students to retain the new word and to learn how to spell it.

Fill in the blanks are also good for grammar exercsies. Have your students fill in just one word for lower levels, but when you get to more complicated verb tenses, for example, have your students fill in two or three verb forms to complete a sentence (or maybe a paragraph). For instance, if your students are working on the present perfect progressive tense, a fill in the blank activity can encourage them to think carefully through all three parts of the verb form.

Cloze Exercises

Cloze exercises are another form of fill in the blank exercises that can be used at all levels. They can be used for dictation activities in which the teacher or perhaps an online video actor speaks, and students write down the missing words in the blanks. This is a close listening activity as well as a spelling exercise.

Cloze activities can also be used for longer texts in which students need to fill in a particular word. Have your students fill in vocabulary words from a text, perhaps choosing from two forms of a word to further challenge them (i.e., between the noun and the adjective forms). You can also choose a cloze activity that focuses just on one grammar point that your students are working on.

The Breaking News English website is one fantastic source for cloze exercises. It is a site full of news articles and cloze activities (and many other kinds as well!) that are available for beginners, intermediate, and advanced students.

Quizzes

Online quizzes with fun animation are not the only way to see if your students have mastered one of your lessons. You can create your own quizzes in your whiteboard program. You might choose from a variety of testing methods and layouts to engage your students and to check their understanding of lesson material.

For example, you might create a multiple choice quiz for your students. If your students are lower-level readers in English (and/or in their native language), consider creating one question per page. Keep a lot of whitespace around the question, and use an image or two to brighten the page (but that doesn't give the answer away).

Be sure that your students understand how to complete the activities in the quiz and that they have practiced that type of activity a few times before. You don't want to give students a matching activity on the quiz that they have never seen before.

If you don't want to create your own quizzes, don't forget that you can use online ESL quizzes as well. Use share screen or shared web browsing, if possible.

Word Searches

Several free online word search creators are available so that you can make a fun activity for your student that helps them practice new vocabulary. This can be entertaining at the end of a text-, audio-, or video-based lesson in which your students were introduced to new words. Word searches are a good way to practice discriminating letters and spelling.

Role Plays

Giving your students authentic speaking practice is essential to their developing their oral skills in English. The online whiteboard is the perfect place to practice role plays. Your students will be able to perfect their sentence and word stress, speaking fluency, intonation, pronunciation, reading skills, and reading with emotion, among other skills when they use role plays.

Design your own role plays that give your students practice with new words or grammar structures/functions they have learned. Another option is to use one of the many free online ESL role plays available. For more advanced students, you might even use a reader's theatre script.

You can find transcripts for radio and podcast stories and interviews on news sites like National Public Radio and BBC Learning English, and online videos often have transcripts as well. Video clips from movies are also readily available online with transcripts.

If you have more than one student, your students might create their own role play together. For example, they might write a short role play about how to order coffee at a coffee shop or ask for directions to the university's registration office. When your students can take ownership of their work, and creatively demonstrate their work, they are more engaged.

If just you and one student are practicing or writing a role play, encourage your student to do most of the writing on the whiteboard. Also encourage him to lead the discussion about the topic or characters in the role play. Additionally, switch roles at least once as you read the role play together so your student is able to practice both parts. Finally, have fun with the activity by using imitative voices for the characters, smile, and laugh through the process to decrease any anxiety your student may be feeling about speaking out loud, or reading/writing in English.

6

Reading Long Documents or Books

Working through long documents such as journal articles or books available online with your students takes a considerable amount of time. The activity can, however, spur several types of activities, such as writing and speaking practice. Before you get started teaching long documents online, work through the technical aspects first so that you and your students can focus just on the text.

Technical Considerations

Be sure that your interactive whiteboard program can handle the number of pages or the size of the document you are uploading. Some programs, like Scribblar, which I currently use, have a page limit per document. Each page is uploaded as a slide. You may not be restricted on the number of slides you have, though.

You might be able to get around this limitation, however, if your document is particularly long or large. One idea is to purchase a PDF to Word/text conversion program. This would allow you to then copy and paste the maximum number of pages into a few documents that you would then need to upload separately into your whiteboard program. (Be sure that the program you choose is safe! Do your research before you decide which one to download.)

Sometimes, you can copy and paste PDF text into a word processing document, but then you have to go through each page and fix all of the formatting errors that occur. This can be a waste of time and money for you if you plan to read long documents with your students regularly. It might be better to invest in a conversion program, as I mentioned before.

Another option is to upload the document (PDF or word processor-produced) to Google Docs, DropBox or a similar file-sharing site. You would then need to share a link to the document with students. Make sure you select the option when you share the document that the students are able to edit it. Otherwise, they won't be able to annotate it. This decreases their interaction during lessons and makes the lesson less engaging and useful.

Google Docs allows you to make comments in the margins and highlight sections of text. The program keeps track of who makes what comments. One thing I like to do with my students is have them highlight new vocabulary words as we read through a text so we can discuss it.

I am currently working with a student where we are doing just that. The text is a bit above his reading level, but he is really interested it. There are often times he does not know several words on a page. I will read a few pages out loud (We take turns.), and he highlights as I read. When it is his turn, he will do the same. I will then write a brief definition for the word in the margins so he can refer to it later if he wishes. We also create vocabulary charts for one of the words each lesson (which I discuss in detail below) to help him remember the new words.

Additionally, shared web browsing in a web conferencing program may allow you and your students to read the same document from a particular website. This is not ideal, however, as the text will be small and may be difficult to read. You and your students also cannot highlight or comment as you can if you use Google Docs or upload the document to the whiteboard.

You could also share your screen with your students through Skype or through this feature in the web conferencing program. This is also not the option of choice because it can be hard for your students to read. If you are sharing it right from your web browser, you will also not be able to make notes, highlight, or save the document for future study.

Whether or not you and your students can study a particular long text in the whiteboard part of the online classroom, make a slide just to keep track of vocabulary words for future study. You can also save a slide so that your students can write written summaries or for explanations of parts of the text that you write out. You or your students could also draw pictures to help them remember what occurred in the text. Use the chat box or a slide to make a note of what page number or chapter you left off for the next class as well. If you use the whiteboard or Google Docs, you can also highlight the line you last read. In the classroom, you could just draw a line under the last line you read together.

7

Vocabulary

One of the best parts of using an online whiteboard is teaching and learning vocabulary. The possibilities to learn vocabulary are just about limitless with this technology. Here are a few ideas to help you get started.

Vocabulary Charts

One popular classroom activity is to create vocabulary charts for each word students learn. Folding a piece of paper in fourths, students use each quadrant to apply the new word in a different way. This helps them to remember the word better than just by writing a list of words and definitions.

In the online whiteboard, the idea is nearly the same. First, students draw a "t" to split the slide into four parts. This can be done with the line drawing tool in the program, or freehand with the pencil tool. The pencil tool is messier, however. Next, students write the word in the area where the two lines intersect.

In the upper left quadrant, students label the box "definition." They then write a definition that is meaningful to them, not a definition straight out of the dictionary that contains more words they don't know. They can use a dictionary to look up the word initially, but encourage them to put the definition into their own words. Students should also write down the part of speech. Focus on the particular definition used in the text you read in which the word came up. If there is more than one definition, you can teach it in a different vocabulary chart.

The students then label the upper right quadrant, "synonym." The students then use Thesaurus.com or another similar site to identify a suitable synonym. You may need to help your students identify a synonym that is close to the meaning of the word being studied. You don't want your students to write "weird" if they are studying the word "psychotic," for example.

In the lower left quadrant, students label the box "antonym," and identify an antonym, which can also often be found on Thesaurus.com. Know that there may not always be a single word antonym or synonym for every word. Explain that to your student. There may not even be a suitable antonym for every word.

Finally, in the lower right-hand quadrant, the students label the box "example/picture." Here, students write an example sentence that uses the word. Many times students have trouble writing a sentence that correctly uses the definition's part of speech. For example, one of my students had difficulty using "malevolence" as a noun. He wanted to change it to "malevolent" several times.

The last part of filling in this box is for your student to draw or find an online image (providing credit to the source, even if it has a Creative Commons license) to illustrate the word. Some students are more visual learners, and this can help them to better remember the word and how to use it in the future.

Other Vocabulary Activities

One method of increasing your students' vocabulary is to write a sentence on the whiteboard, underlining key words for which there are plenty of good synonyms. Have students rewrite the sentence using new words for the underlined words. You might also have them change the sentence to the opposite meaning by adding/taking away words, rearranging the sentence, and using antonyms. This activity idea comes from the Grand Canyon University ESL page, and it is called vertical sentences.

Another way to practice vocabulary is to have your students use the word out loud in a sentence. You might also give your students one or two sentences that use a couple of words as a noun/verb/adjective and then ask them to identify the part of speech. You could do the same for multiple meaning words by writing or speaking sentences that use the word's different meanings. The students would then identify which meaning you intended for each sentence.

If you need to just provide a quick definition, sometimes sharing a screen with your students or using shared browsing can be helpful. Find an image of the word online to quickly share. You can also upload the image to the whiteboard, but this might take a bit of time as you will need to download it to your computer and then upload it, as well as share the link to it.

You can create fill in the blank exercises with or without word banks, use Quizlet or another similar vocabulary flash card site with games and activities through share screen or shared web browsing. You might also create a word search or crossword puzzle online. Vary up the activities that you do to help your students learn new vocabulary.

Another important point is to practice the same vocabulary every lesson. This takes up lesson time, but repeated exposure to a word is essential if a student is going to learn it well. I have my students who read texts choose just one or two words each lesson to add to their growing list of vocabulary charts in the online whiteboard. The program Scribblar saves whatever we write on the board, so it is available for the next class.

My students look at each vocabulary chart as we review during the lesson. They can see the definition and examples of how to use the word. However, I ask them to then create a sentence using the word that is different than the one that they wrote for the example/picture quadrant. I just have them speak this out loud most of the time, but you could also have them write the sentence out on the whiteboard and then erase it before moving on to the next vocabulary slide.

8

Activities for Reading

Before You Read

Activate your students' current knowledge of the subject about which you're going to read together. You can do this by asking questions about what they already know about the topic. Have them write anything they can think of on the whiteboard around a word you write on the screen that relates to the central theme or idea of the text. For example, if you are reading The Giver by Lois Lowry together, you might write "sameness" in the middle of the screen, and let students write whatever they can think of that relates to the word around it.

You could also activate your students' knowledge by putting up an image related to the topic on the whiteboard (with proper attribution), and ask your students what comes to mind.

Get your students talking about the topic in whatever way you can. Watch a short video about it, being sure that you frontload students with any new vocabulary in the video and have subtitles up if necessary, depending on their language level. You might also write some thought-provoking questions on the board that get students to think creatively and deeply about the text's topic. If you were teaching The Giver, you might write "How would you react if you had to apologize for everything you did, no matter how minor? What would you think if you had to wear the same clothes and have the same haircut as everyone else in your community? Would you want someone else to pick out your life career for you? Why or why not?"

KWL Chart

Another way to engage your readers before you start reading is to create a "KWL" chart together. This is a commonly-used classroom tool created by Donna Ogle in 1986, according to TeachingHistory.org, in which students split a piece of paper into three vertical columns. "K" stands for "know," or "what I already know" about the topic. Here students can write what knowledge they already have.

In the next column, students write what they "want" to know, hence the "W" in "KWL." This helps them identify a purpose for reading. They must carefully consider what the book or text is about by skimming it – looking at the title, headlines, pictures, graphics, and captions – and then decide what kind of information the text might provide. They then select information they think they may learn based on that criteria.

After students read, they fill in the "L" column, which stands for "learned." In this column, students write down what they learned after they read. This is a good place for them to see if the predictions about what they hoped to learn based on their initial reading of the text were accurate. It also helps them recap and summarize what the text was about.

This activity can easily be adapted to the online whiteboard, and students are engaged in this activity through writing, speaking, perhaps uploading pictures of what they learned, what they hope to learn, and about what they already know about the topic.

As You Read

Checking your students' understanding of a text is essential as you read. You can do this in a number of ways, depending on your students' learning style preferences, age, attention span, langugage skills, etc.

Bloom's Taxonomy

Bloom's taxonomy is a helpful guide to get your students thinking critically about what they read. At the top of the taxonomy are simple identification and recall activities that help your students check and amend their understanding of the text. Deeper, more critical thinking activities can help your students to analyze, interpret, examine, and create based on ideas they read in the text.

Ask your students to summarize the text every page or two out loud. Vary this activity by having them write a quick paragraph about what happened in the text. You could also give a summary yourself with a missing or incorrect piece and have your students identify what should be changed and how. For your intermediate and beginner students, provide sentence starters on the screen for both conversation- and writing-oriented summarization activities.

Another idea is to have students answer questions you place to them about what happens in the text. Prepare these questions ahead of time to maximize learning time. You can often find discussion questions or online quizzes for books or plays. Use these free resources, but be sure you give credit to them if you use them on your whiteboard.

Lower-level students could also draw pictures of what happened in the text, and then explain it out loud. This would also be an appropriate activity for intermediate and advanced students. Just enhance the amount and type of discussion you require from them (i.e., higher-level vocabulary, more complex sentence structure, wider use of verb tenses).

Also, have your students predict what will happen next in the text. They could do this out loud, or they could write a paragraph, or draw an image. They might also find an image online, attribute the source, and then upload it to the whiteboard. If they do a drawing, they should discuss it out loud or with written text, the difficulty of their writing depending on their age, level, etc. Periodically revisit students' predictions to see if they were correct. Keep track of predictions on a particular slide on the whiteboard or by writing comments in the margins of the text in Google Docs.

You could also have your students role play characters' dialogue from a particular section of the story while you are reading. If you have more than one student in the class, this is a good way for them to practice speaking. Put up the text from that section of the story, and have them practice it. Students might also work out a dialogue for what they think will happen next to a couple of characters, or write an alternate ending for a chapter using dialogue. If you teach one-on-one, you can be your student's partner as you complete these activities.

Similar to the "W" column in the "KWL" chart activity, you can also have students write what questions they have on each page or every few pages of text in the online whiteboard or in Google Docs in the comments. This is an adaptation of a classroom exercise from the Edge series of ESL books by Moore, et al. National Geographic published in 2007 in which students use sticky notes to write their questions. Have them write answers to the questions they wrote if they find them. Encourage students to preview each page if there are headlines, graphics, captions, etc. to help them write more accurate questions.

After You Read

When your students are finished reading a text, use Bloom's taxonomy to create projects or exercises that help them to think critically about the text. They might create a Prezi, which is a fun way to create Internet-based presentations. You can have your students sign up with a free account, or they could use your account. Tell students that their Prezis are public, unless you or they pay for a subscription. That way, they don't put up personal information. Ideas for creating a Prezi might include:

- What engaged you most about the text?
- How would you have personally solved the main conflict in the text?
- Create an alternate ending for the story.
- Relate this story to your own life. Choose a theme and connect it with your own life experience. (Be sure to discuss themes and topics prevalent in the text first.)

You might have students write an argumentative essay using textual and outside evidence as well. Use the text as a jumping-off point to teach a unit on writing a research paper.

Another idea is to have students interview someone in their families, circle of friends or acquaintances, or someone in their communities who has knowledge about a theme or topic related to the text. Students would develop a set of questions first, contact the person, set up a meeting time, and do the interview. They could then record the audio or the video of the interview with the interviewee's permission and share it with the class and/or you in the web conferencing program.

These are just a few ideas to get you and your students started on how to culminate the reading of a long document or text. Let your students' passions, talents, and preferences guide your lesson. That is the beauty of teaching ESL online.

Other Reading Activities

To practice oral reading fluency, have your student pick a paragraph from the text. You read it out loud, timing yourself, perhaps with your smartphone's stop watch. Write the time on the board so the students know how long it might take a native speaker to read it. Tell the student to read it themselves to see how long it takes them. Time them as they read. Write that down as well.

Help students learn to link words together, pronounce words correctly, to reduce them, use contractions, and to place correct syllable and word emphasis in sentences. This will help them to speed up their reading. Read each sentence to your student. Have your students then repeat the line. Read the next line, and have the students read that line. Then you read the first two lines, and have your students read the first two lines. Keep doing this until you and your student are reading the entire paragraph. Time your students two more times, and keep track of the times. Then your students may enjoy seeing a quick line graph you create of how much faster they got as they did this exercise.

You can also record your students' voice reading the paragraph as you work through it. Do this with your computer's sound recorder or your smart phone's recording app. Unplug your headset (just the speaker plug if you have the older two-plug system on your computer), and turn your computer's volume all the way up. Hold the microphone of the headset if you have the older two-plug system to your speakers, or put your phone right up to your computer's speakers. This is not as good as having your students record themselves on their computers, phones, or tablets, however.

Save the recording (or have your students save the recording), and then play it back for your students (or have them play it back so you can hear it). I would suggest that you or your students record all three readings. At the end of the exercise, play the first and last recordings. Have students identify their own errors this way. Also encourage them to identify what they did well.

If you are teaching a pronunciation class, pre-select a paragraph from a text that contains several sounds with which your students struggle. You might even write your own paragraph that contains these sounds.

Adaptability

I understand that some of these activities are not necessarily feasible if you teach online with an online tutoring company in which lessons are already planned for you. However, you can adapt some of them, such as previewing the text, writing predictions, etc. to suit your particular teaching situation.

9

Activities for Speaking

Getting your students to speak during the lesson is one of the most important tasks you have as an online ESL teacher. I would say the majority of ESL students who take classes online want to improve their conversational skills. Your job is to get them to talk at least 80 percent of the time, while you only speak twenty percent.

Discussion Questions

Create a list of ice breaker or conversation questions to use with your students. You might find conversations starters online or even in a game format. I personally have used some cards in the form of a family dinner table conversation game I found with one of my students. Each class, have your students formulate a response to these questions. If your students are preparing for a test like the IELTS or TOEFL in which they will be required to speak at length, intersperse the general conversation questions with authentic test questions they may face. Furthermore, give your students just a minute or two to write down notes to answer the questions. You might also have them draw a picture to illustrate their thoughts about a certain question. For instance, I had one of my students draw the superhero she wanted to be and then explain to me the hero's features and why she wanted to be that hero.

Encourage your students to use transition words like "first," "next," and "finally." Time them, and graph their progress. Students will be excited to see how much longer they can confidently speak in English over time.

Two Truths and a Lie

While this activity won't get your students speaking for long lengths of time, it is a fun warm-up. Have students say and write on the board two truths about themselves and one lie. Other students have to guess which one is the lie. You can do it over the course of a few classes, giving points out each time students guess correctly.

Holidays from Hell

Posted on Dave's ESL Café website by Gareth, this activity splits students into two groups. One student tells a story of a bad holiday she has experienced, and this student has to convince the other students that some sort of compensation is in order. You can pair students up and have them work in a breakout session room, and then present their case to hotel managers, airline representatives, etc.

ESL Teachers Share Speaking Activity Ideas Online

I could list dozens of activities for speaking and listening, but, honestly, searching online is the best. I love Dave's ESL Café, where teachers upload ideas to use in their classrooms on a regular basis. I have used "Two Truths and a Lie" with one of my students. This activity provided writing practice in the simple past tense, listening, and speaking practice.

Current Event Discussion

After reading a current event story or a short text of another type together, have your students create their own discussion questions to delve deeper into the topic. You can also create some questions for them. Opinion questions in which students have to state their opinion clearly and then support it with evidence or reasons is very good practice for having conversations in English, particularly in an academic environment. If you have more than one student, encourage them to talk to one another, listening carefully, and then have them follow up with other questions.

10

Listening Activities

Listening to Each Other

Have students present a speech on a topic or describe what they did over the weekend. See if another student can summarize what was said. Ask students to develop questions to ask that require the speaker to provide more information. Writing these questions and asking them requires that the listening student has a good understanding of what was said. This also encourages conversation skills.

Videos and Podcasts

In the resources section in the appendix, you'll find various sites that offer news articles students can listen to, videos from movies, commercials, and actual ESL videos. Many of them offer quizzes following the recording if the site is geared toward ESL learners.

Test Preparation

If your students are preparing for a test like the IELTS or TOEFL, use online listening test materials to help them practice. Have them work through entire listening tests under as-close-to-real testing conditions as you can create in an online environment. This will help them prepare for the kinds of recordings that they will have to hear when they actually take the test.

Perking Up Pronunciation

In an activity submitted by Paul Careless to Dave's ESL Café's listening section, students are encouraged to repeat as much of a level-appropriate recording as possible. They can record themselves reading a text and then try to repeat as much of it as they can. They can also listen to audio from videos, podcasts, or the teacher reading. They might also try to listen to recordings other students play during the class through their external speakers at a high volume and repeat what they hear. Online streaming radio might also work. They can then improve their pronunciation, intonation, and fluency by playing the recordings and repeating them several times.

Dictation

Dictation is another good listening exercise for students. This is explained in further detail below, but the basic idea is to choose a text that is appropriate to the level of your students and then read it. They can also use other recordings found online. They then write down what they hear. This also helps them improve their vocabulary, grammar and spelling.

11

Writing Activities

Online Sharing and Correction Forum or Blog

Each week, have your students respond to a journal prompt that you provide or that one of your students provides. Students then respond to the prompt in an online forum or blog format (using one of the many free website builders available, like those from Google), and they correct each other's writing and offer responses. Students might respond to literature they are reading with you this way as well.

Smile! Write Poetry with Similes!

This activity is offered by Jassica Chang on Dave's ESL Café writing section. Provide students an introduction to similes. Then provide an opening line from which they can build their own similes, such as "Friendship is. . ." Then, removing all the prepositions and unnecessary words, the teacher puts students' submissions on the board, creating a communal poem. Students can write their responses on the whiteboard, and the teacher can move the text objects into place after editing them to remove extra words while each student finishes writing.

Pass the Story

Adapting the "Pass the Story" idea offered by Chris on Dave's ESL Café's writing section, you can start a story with one sentence and have each student write another sentence to add onto it. You could save the story from class to class, and the story could be a good warm-up. These stories can be really funny and entertaining. You might stipulate that students write only in a specific tense, on a certain theme, or use new vocabulary words that the class has been studying to make the story more relevant to what students are learning.

Re-Writing a Story as a Script

Either working with your individual student or putting your students in pairs or small groups, have your students rewrite a short story as a script. Consider the number of characters plus a narrator as you build the groups. This idea comes from Cliff Pfeil on Dave's ESL Café writing section. Students then perform the script in a Reader's Theatre format, which gives them reading and speaking practice. You can also have students in the audience write down as much as they remember from the story on the whiteboard as a listening and writing exercise.

12

Games

Games that are relevant to your ESL lesson are great review activities for students. They also help you see if your students have mastered a concept. Through screen share or shared web browsing, you and your students can break the monotony of reading and writing. Games help lighten the mood of the classroom and inject some often much-needed humor.

Jeopardy

To test your students' knowledge of a grammar concept, content of a text, or other material you're teaching, you can create a Jeopardy game with PowerPoint or with free, online Jeopardy game creators. This is fun with a group class as well. Split the class up into teams, and let the fun begin. You will need to be in control of turning the "cards" over for students, but another option is to assign someone from a small group class to be the host.

Pictionary

Draw an image on the whiteboard that represents a vocabulary word students have been practicing. Give your students three guesses to get the word correct. You can also adapt this to a group. Each team would get a chance to identify a particular word. If one team gets a word incorrect, the other has a chance to guess it. Keep track of the points on the board, and let the teams choose their names.

Hang Man

Hang Man is another fun game for students. It is fun for vocabulary words and even for longer groups of words like idioms or sentences. You might make up a particular grammar form that students have to guess as well. If you are practicing direct and indirect question forms (or formal or informal vocabulary, for that matter), you could use that in Hang Man, too.

Word Scramble

Create a list of about five to ten vocabulary words in the same general category (animals, greeting expressions, vocabulary about business emails, etc.). Scramble the letters for each word and instruct students to unscramble the letters. They will practice spelling and vocabulary recall during this exercise. To add an element of competition, use a timer to see how long it takes them to complete it. If you are teaching a small class, say, of two to four students, open up a different workspace in the whiteboard program to allow them to work together in pairs or small groups on the word scramble. The first team who writes "Done!" in the group chat box and has spelled everything correctly wins.

You can also pit students against each other individually, having them write down their answers to the word scramble on the whiteboard in different colors in an organized list. The first one to complete the activity and write his/her words on the whiteboard correctly wins. Or the student who has the most words complete after a set amount of time, say, a couple of minutes, wins.

Another option is to use sharescreen to complete categorically-organized word scrambles online. These activities are already created for you, and they make use of Flash plugins or perhaps Java that make them more interesting for students than static words on a whiteboard. Note that this works best for one-on-one tutoring, and that students and you should have the appropriate browser plug-ins enabled to be able to see these games.

Sentence Scramble

Similar to word scramble activities, a sentence scramble game helps students practice syntax. Write words on the whiteboard in random order from a sentence. Vary the complexity of the sentence based on the level of your students. For example, sentences with subject, verb, object structure would be most appropriate for beginning students, but compound or complex sentences would be good for intermediate/advanced students.

Incorporate grammar structures that you are studying into each sentence you have students unscramble. This reinforces the grammar point and gives students extra practice. For instance, if you work with beginning students, you might make each sentence a "Wh-" question.

To make things more challenging, consider putting up words for two sentences on the board. Ensure that the wording of the sentences does not allow for confusion about which words go with which sentences.

For more advanced students, create entire paragraph scrambles using an online generator to make your preparation work easier.

Syntax Surgery

Another fun activity from Grand Canyon University ESL is called Syntax Surgery. Write a list of words from a sentence that matches your students' learning level and your lesson's grammar objectives on the whiteboard. Have students work quickly in small groups or individually to identify the parts of speech for each word and write the part of speech next to each word in the list. They should then match subjects and verbs, deciding which are okay combinations.

Then they can move on to possessive adjectives and adjectives, putting them with nouns and verbs. Next, they can identify prepositions, and put nouns and prepositions together. Finally, they can decide what the object(s) is/are, and put the sentences together. This is a more structured and systematic approach to the sentence scramble exercise that encourages students to carefully consider each step of building a sentence in English. Timing students keeps them on their toes and makes the activity into a game.

Dictation

Dictatation is not just a boring listening comprehension exercise. Turn it into a game to practice punctuation, spelling, and vocabulary by making the dictations funny to hear. Almost any text can work for a dictation exercise, although plenty of exercises specifically for dictation can be found online or in ESL textbooks.

Have students write down what they think they hear on paper at home, and then have them write their answers on the whiteboard at the same time. The class can then enjoy each other's written renditions of the dictation. After that, they can identify errors and correct them when you read the dictation again, and write the correct answer on the board. Again, try to make the dictation text relevant thematically (for new vocabulary and expansion of subject knowledge) and grammatically to your current topic of langauge study.

13

Videos

Videos are perfect for the online classroom. They provide students with authentic conversations to model, cultural information (from the clothes actors wear to the way greetings are carried out), listening and grammar practice, and new vocabulary words and expressions. They also liven up lessons that may be heavily text-based.

Tips for Using Videos

1. Keep the Clips Short.

Avoid overwhelming your students with videos that are too long. Students may lose interest, stop listening, or get overloaded with new words to understand what is going on. Long videos simply take time away from teaching.

2. Have a Teaching Point.

There should be a clear point to watching each video with students. Tell them up front what they are watching and listening for. Is it the use of a particular verb tense, vocabulary you've gone over in class, a dictation/listening exercise? They should understand that there is a purpose for watching the video before you hit play.

3. Clips Should Be Audience-Appropriate.

You're not going to want to show an adult-rated film clip to students who are in middle school, no matter how relevant the dialogue is to what you're teaching. Even if the clip is innocuous, students will want to know what movie it's from. Then they may find a way to watch the movie. You could be looking at some upset parents if you introduce them to a film that is not appropriate. Also consider gender, overall culture, individual personalities of your students, etc. before you settle on a clip to complement your lesson.

Role Plays

Whether you and your students watch a clip from a commercial or movie, or one of the many videos made just for ESL students to watch online, videos are the perfect way to introduce a role play activity. They serve as examples for pronunciation, intonation, vocabulary, organization of speech, and grammar.

After your students watch a video, have them act out the dialogue they watched in pairs or small groups. Of course, this will likely be a dialogue-only role play done through microphones in the online classrooms, but students can adopt inflected voices to imitate characters or otherwise experiment with creatively presenting their scene. They might practice it a few times in a whiteboard breakout room and then present it to the rest of the class.

Additionally, students could vary the conversation they hear in the video by rewriting the dialogue in a different verb tense, writing the next scene based on what they think will happen and perform it, or otherwise embellish the role play. Keep the creativity contained and centered around the lesson you're teaching, however.

14

Images

Students often have questions about what a particular word means during class. In an online environment, it is easy to quickly show them. Sometimes pictures do more to explain a concept or object than words do. Simply use on online search engine like Google's image search to find the word, and then send the link to the student. Be careful, however, because some words come up with inappropriate images. You may need to add/delete a word or two from your search to get the image that you need to send to your student. You can share the link via Skype chat, whiteboard classroom chat, shared web browsing if your whiteboard program supports it, via share screen in Skype, or through the share screen feature in your online classroom.

Images can be also be quickly added to an empty whiteboard for a warm-up to learn vocabulary, a writing exercise, or as conversation starters. If you have been learning vocabulary related to the image, ask students what they see in the picture. Have them explain it to you in detail. How much detail depends on their language level, of course. Practice using grammar that has been practiced before, or to introduce a new language function or grammar point.

To share an image with your students, just download an Internet image to share with your student and then upload it to the classroom. Copy and paste the URL of the image so that students know the source as well. This can take a couple of minutes to accomplish, so try to complete the process before your online class starts.

15

Making the Most of Whiteboard Space

You will probably use a PowerPoint or Word document that you upload to the whiteboard for your lessons. You may also choose to make your slides or screens ahead of time in the online classroom if the program you use has the capability to save your material from one class to the next.

Note that many online whiteboards, especially the free ones, do not allow you to save your documents or materials over time. Students cannot go back into the classroom to take screenshots or complete assignments, and you cannot prepare your lessons beforehand. Many whiteboard programs (especially the free ones) are "just-in-time," meaning you can only create what you want to use for a lesson when you are in a previously scheduled virtual whiteboard classroom.

If you use the whiteboard to create your lessons (whether it's a just-in-time program or one in which you can save materials before class to the whiteboard), remember the volatility of the Internet and that you can lose the material by some freak accident. Hence, you will likely want to prepare your lessons using one PowerPoint or Word ahead of time and save them to your computer and/or to an external hard drive or to a cloud (online storage like Google Drive, DropBox, or one of the many others offered by individual companies for a fee or for free).

Many whiteboard programs will also allow you to upload image or PDF files.

If you do use PowerPoint or Word to create your lessons before each class, pay close attention to your use of images, text, and white space. They can affect how well your students understand and remember your lesson.

- Use no more than about nine or ten words per line if you create slides in Power Point or if you are providing instruction in Word. Use only two or three bullet points per page.

- If you use images, ensure they are culturally and age-appropriate and that they don't detract from any text on the slide or page. Use at least one image every two pages as students can get tired looking at a screen with just words on it.

- Use large font sizes as small fonts (often under size 16 or 14) can be difficult to read when they are uploaded to the whiteboard. Also use dark, bold colors that are easy to see and a font that is simple to read (Times New Roman, Calibri – anything without too many curly cues or that is in cursive) You may need to put text in bold as well so that students can see it more easily. Remember that you may need to do this in PowerPoint or Word (or a similar program, like Google's slide tool or word processor you can share directly with your students via a link) before you upload it to the classroom.

- Use large margins. Remember: white space is your friend. It doesn't matter that your document or file has thirty pages or slides. What is important is that your students can read it and understand it easily. When the document is uploaded, each page or slide will become an individual page or slide in the whiteboard.

- Some whiteboard programs only allow you to upload images. If this is the case, you may need to take a screen shot of each page, save it to your hard drive, and then upload each page individually. Double check what types of files you can upload into your whiteboard program, and give yourself plenty of time to change file type, take screenshots, etc. before your classes.

- Note that if you are creating a document with a lot of pages, it may become a large document that is too unwieldy to upload. Double check the size of the document that can be uploaded before you make the final touches to your document, image, or slide show. You may need to save it as more than one document and then upload them separately.

16

Recording Lessons

Some whiteboards may allow you to record lessons. This is a great feature that allows students and you to review information presented during the lesson. Students can save the file and review it before a test, to help them complete their homework, or just for extra study on their own time.

You can use it to check the quality of your lessons. If students say they are dissatisfied with a lesson for any reason, you can review the lesson yourself. The recording serves as evidence. It can also be helpful for you to review your own lessons from time to time to see where you can improve the flow or presentation of a lesson.

You can also review them to remind yourself what you covered last week. This can help you prepare for the next lesson. Perhaps you notice when you review last week's lesson for a particular student, for example, that she had some trouble with a particular concept. For next week's lesson, you can provide extra practice for her.

You can also buy software that will let you record the audio and visual images from the lesson. Skype's help website has a list of third-party call and video recording providers you can try. You can then email your students lesson recordings after the lesson, or you can upload it to a shared file location, such as Google Drive or DropBox.

17

Error Correction

Students need immediate feedback on errors, but it needs to be delivered with professionalism and courtesy.

In an online environment, you will likely find that you will need to do a bit more waiting than you are used to in a traditional classroom as the lag time between when the student finishes talking and when you think he finishes talking can sometimes be a few seconds. If you speak too soon, you can end up interrupting the student, which can increase students' level of frustration in practicing speaking in English.

Use clarifying questions to see when a student is finished reading, talking, or finishing a written exercise on the whiteboard. Here are some you might use:

- I see that you have written several sentences. Do you need some more time to finish the paragraph, or are you ready to move on? (for written exercises)

- I want to make sure I'm not interrupting you. Were you finished speaking? (for speaking/listening exercises) This can also be helpful for online classes with more than one student when students need to speak together.

- Let me know when you are done reading the text. Then we can move on to the next activity when you're ready. (for reading exercises)

Here are a few other error correction techniques you may find helpful.

- Restate what your students said or wrote with a questioning tone to see if they can identify their own mistakes.

- Use the whiteboard highlighter or pointer to highlight students' mistakes to see if they can self-correct.

- Only correct a few errors, especially those that relate to the lesson topic. Avoid correcting every error as it can demoralize students.

- Remember to offer specific praise of what students did well.

- Provide your students with think time when you ask them a question. Remember the lag time issue that often happens with audio and video conferencing.

- Type what your students say, and have them find their own mistakes. You can also rewrite the paragraph with corrections.

18

Teaching Students to Use a Whiteboard Effectively

Students will likely experience a learning curve when they use the online whiteboard and classroom. Even if they are experienced in taking classes online, they must still learn the particularities of the program you are using.

Use the first several minutes of your first class pointing out the basic tools your students will likely use at some point. You might schedule a training class to allow your students time to get used to the tools and to teach them how to use them without the pressure of taking time away from the first lesson. You can do this through screen share, perhaps using Skype as your initial voice and video tool before you use the one the whiteboard provides.

Focus on the basic tools like how to write text, the high-lighter, creating shapes, changing font size/type/color, deleting an object or text from the screen, turning video and audio on and off, using the chat box, raising a hand to ask a question, using the polling feature or emoticons if the program offers them, drawing pencil, how to share screens, etc. Your students may do not need to know how to upload documents, but they may if you intend to have them upload images during lessons or share files of work they have created. You can also teach other utilities on an as-needed basis.

Students can use these tools for a variety of purposes. For example, they can highlight a word in a text you're reading out loud to indicate that they don't understand the word without interrupting you. They can also use the text and chat box features to write down words they are saying for which you cannot understand their prounnunciation. They may also need to know how to use the shared web browser, how to share screens, and how to use the drawing tool to show you an image of a word they need help pronouncing or that they want to know how to say in English.

Know How to Use the Whiteboard Yourself

Make sure you are very familiar with how to use the whiteboard program yourself before you have your first lesson with students. You will need to be able to send them links to the classroom, and passwords and usernames if your program requires students to have them. You should understand the differences between student and moderator status as well. Moderators can generally control whether a student can write on the board, talk, or whether her video is on. This is important as technological problems or an overzealous student may require you to turn off some of their capabilities.

You should also know and be able to pay attention to the chat box, monitor student emoticons and whether they are raising their hands if they have a question in the participant box. These are ways students will try to communicate with you if they have a question or technical problem. They may also express confusion or frustration, and this information can help you refocus your lesson according to their needs.

Spend plenty of time in the online classroom using all of the features that you will need. This will enable you to explain how to use them to your students. You also need to have the email, IM screen name (and the specific IM program tech support uses installed on your computer with a username and password already set up before your first lesson if you're teaching for an online ESL tutoring company), phone number, or other contact information for tech support if your whiteboard program provides it. Try to help your students solve their own problems before you contact tech support to save time.

19

Classroom Management

Managing an online classroom requires a different set of skills than a traditional classroom, but the main goal is the same: to keep your students focused and learning throughout the class. Making your classroom run smoothly online is not really that hard, but it does take some practice, and plenty of confidence. If you've already taught in a traditional classroom, the latter quality should come easily. If not, then practice will help you develop it quickly.

Pacing

Just as in a regular classroom, students get bored if they have to spend too long doing one type of activity. You want your students to practice listening, reading, writing, and speaking in each lesson, if possible. This opens up many doors so that you can use a variety of activities in your lessons. Try to change your activities up at least every fifteen to twenty minutes. This will provide around a few transitions for your students in a 45-minute or hour-long class. Some activities may only take five minutes, while others may take much longer.

Ask your students for feedback on whether a particular lesson provided enough different types of activities when class finishes. This will help you hone your lessons to meet the particular learning styles and needs of your students.

For Classes with Two/Three or More Students

When your online classes get larger than just one or two students, you may need to start using more class management tools. Depending on the students, you may also need them with two students.

- Have students turn off their microphones. This helps prevent feedback especially if students are not using headphones during class.

- Tell students to use the chat box or to raise their hands if they have questions or comments so as not to interrupt other students.

- Teach students to use emoticons, the thumbs up sign, clapping symbol, etc. to share emotions in class instead of speaking when others are talking.

- Enable students to write on the board when it is their turn to practice in class.

- Have students work in small groups in breakout sessions or open different tabs/whiteboards for students to work on simultaneously, if your whiteboard program offers these features. This enables students to do small group work and then to come back together as an entire class. If you choose to use this option, make sure you teach students how to turn on and off their mics/video, etc. to prevent and fix technical problems. Move from group to group to ensure students are on task and to answer any questions they have.

20

Presenting Yourself Professionally

Your students count on you to effectively lead each lesson. Here are some tips to help you present yourself in a professional way:

- Use a light-colored, blank wall as a background. Distracting photos or posters can cause your students to ask questions about your wall instead of the lesson. You may also need to hang a light-colored sheet behind you if you don't have a blank wall. Light colors help your students see your face better.

- Make sure your room has enough lighting. Your students need to see your mouth and your face to see how you pronounce words and to see your facial expressions. You may need a lamp or two near your computer.

- Avoid sitting in front of a window as the sunlight can blank your face out on the video stream.

- Wear professional clothes when you teach. Even if you are really sitting in your pajama bottoms, wear a collared shirt to at least appear professional from the shoulders up. Comb or brush your hair, too.

- Show up to class at least fifteen minutes early to handle any last-minute technical problems and to open up the class for your students as they arrive.

- Greet your students as they enter the classroom, but don't waste more than a couple of minutes on this. You might have a fun poll question for them to answer as they come in and then a short discussion on it, like "Which of these activities did you do this last weekend?" Stay focused on the lesson.

- Take charge of your class by watching the clock. Give students time warnings when you are about to move onto the next activity, but also be flexible to not rush ahead when students obviously need more time to finish a task.

- Don't allow one student to dominate the class. If you have students in small groups, ensure that the quieter students can work in a group where they will be heard. Also, lay out the rules of the class from the beginning, letting students know that they are all safe in the class, each contribution is valuable, and that students who dominate discussions are encouraged to let others speak. Turn off microphones of students who talk too much if it becomes necessary.

- Regularly seek feedback from your students about how class went. Which activities did they enjoy/not enjoy? What can you do better?

- **Have fun, and get creative with your lessons!** Try something new from time to time with your students. Vary your activities. Find ways to adapt traditional classroom activities to an online environment.

APPENDIX

Helpful Websites

Debra Garcia's From Private Lessons to a Thriving Business: 10 Steps to a Successful ESL Tutoring Business

http://www.teaching-esl-to-adults.com/how-to-start-esl-tutoring-business.html

She also offers lots of great, free resources on her website.

http://www.teaching-esl-to-adults.com

Teaching ESL Online

This website offers a host of resources and courses to help you set up and build your online ESL business.

http://www.teachingeslonline.com/

Some Whiteboard Options

Scribblar

This is the whiteboard program I currently use for my business.

http://www.scribblar.com/

Educational Technology and Mobile Learning: 7 Awesome Collaborative Whiteboard Tools for Teachers

This site includes a list of free, interactive online whiteboards, as well as some subscription-based services.

http://www.educatorstechnology.com/2012/11/7-awesome-collaborative-whiteboard.html

TutorsBox

Similar to Scribblar, this service is subscription-based, and it offers email reminders and scheduling options for classes in addition to audio and video.

https://tutorsbox.com/en/accounts/register/complete/?email=leyla@empowerenglishtutoring.com

Stoodle

http://stoodle.ck12.org/

This site offers free whiteboard collaboration and permanent storage of classrooms, along with audio and text chat.

E-Learning Queen: Free Online Tutoring Platforms / Open Source Whiteboards – Webinar Platforms

This site offers another list of free, interactive whiteboard services.

http://elearnqueen.blogspot.com/2012/09/free-online-tutoring-platforms-open.html

WyzAnt

This site is one of many tutoring sites that offer teachers the opportunity to connect with students. This is one of the more reputable sites out there, and part of your fees are given to the site for operation fees. There is also the option to use their online whiteboard so that you don't have to pay for your own service. I have used this service myself.

http://www.wyzant.com

University Tutors

This site offers you the chance to connect with students for free who are looking for university-level tutors in a variety of subjects. I have used this site before as well.

http://www.universitytutor.com/

Skooli

Skooli offers online classroom capabilities and a place to find students for tutors. Your visibility as a tutor increases when you submit credentials, and you can schedule your students around your personal schedule.

https://skooli.com/for_tutors

Cloze Exercises and More!

What are ESL Cloze Exercises?

This site explains what cloze exercises are and how to use them in an ESL classroom.

http://www.teaching-esl-to-adults.com/esl-cloze-exer-cises.html

EL Civics

This site offers worksheets for a variety of ESL lessons, and it also has some cloze exercises for students to complete.

http://www.elcivics.com/worksheets/cloze-exercises/printable.html

Boggle World ESL

This site offers cloze exercises, in addition to lots of other activities for ESL students, grouped into holiday, children, and adult classifications.

http://bogglesworldesl.com/cloze_activities.htm

ESL Kids World

According to their website, ESL Kids World offers "high quality printable PDF worksheets for teaching young learners."

http://eslkidsworld.com/worksheets.html

Breaking News English

This is, by far, one of my favorite ESL learning websites. It offers current news stories and follow-up activities for seven different levels of English. Cloze exercises are just one of the MANY great activities this site offers.

http://www.breakingnewsenglish.com/

Using English

This site has some good grammar quizzes for your students to try in addition to language tests, reading comprehension materials, and other teacher materials.

http://www.usingenglish.com/quizzes/

Moby Max

This site offers free and fee-based features for teachers who want to give their students extra practice in the areas of math and language. It offers progress tracking, games, rewards, a placement test, and more!

http://www.mobymax.com

Quizlet

This site allows students to build an online bank of vocabulary words and their meanings in the form of flashcards for free. They can also play games and do a variety of activities to practice the words.

https://quizlet.com/

Jeopardy Game Creators and Templates

Create online Jeopardy games with these sites:

https://www.superteachertools.net/jeopardyx/

https://jeopardylabs.com/

http://www.jeopardy.rocks/

Download PowerPoint Jeopardy templates here:

http://www.edtechnetwork.com/powerpoint.html

Word, Sentence, and Paragraph Scramble Generators

Word:

http://www.superteacherworksheets.com/generator-word-scramble.html

http://worksheets.theteacherscorner.net/make-your-own/word-scramble/

http://search.teach-nology.com/cgi-bin/scramble.pl

http://www.armoredpenguin.com/wordscramble/

Sentence:

http://www.johnsesl.com/scrambler/sent_scr/scr_sent.shtml

http://www.toolsforenglish.com/tools/scramble-sentence/

http://www.altastic.com/scramblinator/

Paragraph:

http://davidbrett.uniss.it/eLearningTools/paragraph%20scrambler.html

http://www.toolsforenglish.com/tools/scramble-paragraphs/

http://www.listenandlearn.org/worksheet-generators/scramble-paragraphs.php

English Page

This website offers comprehensive grammar materials for students to learn and practice grammar, vocabulary, reading, and listening. There are also games. The grammar sections with their quizzes and exercises are my favorite part sof the site.

http://englishpage.com/

A to Z Teacher Stuff

This site offers lots of general teaching worksheets as well as a free word search maker that you can customize for students.

http://tools.atozteacherstuff.com/word-search-maker/wordsearch.php

Super Teacher Worksheets

This site offers inexpensive subscription-based access to a variety of language and reading exercises for students in elementary school. I have successfully used the worksheets with middle and high school students, as well as adults for extra practice.

http://www.superteacherworksheets.com

Thesaurus.com

This site is one my students regularly visit to learn synonyms and antonym for new vocabulary words.

http://www.thesaurus.com

Grand Canyon University ESL

This link is for the vertical sentences activity referenced in the text. There are other great activities on the site as well.

http://gcutesol.weebly.com/you-do-syntax-and-verb-tense.html

Prezi

Prezi offers students (and teachers) an alternate way to make presentations than PowerPoint. It is a fun and free way to share what students have learned or to present a lesson. Note that free account Prezis are public. To make them private, you will need to pay a fee.

http://www.prezi.com

Skype's List of Third Party Call / Video Recorders

https://support.skype.com/en/faq/FA12395/how-can-i-record-my-skype-calls

Busy Teacher

This site provides ESL teachers not only with thousands of pre-made worksheets on a variety of topics, but it also offers great teaching advice articles specifically for ESL.

http://www.busyteacher.org

Video Websites

Some of these sites have actual English lessons. Others have movie, sitcom, and commercial video clips with quizzes afterward, and some are news sites with a variety of English learning material, which includes news videos with transcripts. Many sites have videos split up by language level so you can get the right video for your particular student. Explore them all!

ESL Video

http://www.eslvideo.com/

Real English

http://www.real-english.com/reo/index.asp

Learn English Feel Good

http://www.learnenglishfeelgood.com/eslvideo/

Randall's ESL Lab

http://www.esl-lab.com/videoclips.htm

English Media Lab

http://www.englishmedialab.com/higherlevels.html

Voice of America Learning English

http://learningenglish.voanews.com/

BBC Learning English

http://www.bbc.co.uk/learningenglish

Dictation

http://www.rong-chang.com/eslread/eslread/dict/contents.htm

https://www.englishclub.com/listening/dictation.htm

http://busyteacher.org/classroom_activities-writing/dictations-worksheets/

ESL Teacher's Board

This site offers teachers ways to connect with each other, find jobs online and connect with students who want private tutors.

http://www.eslteachersboard.com/

Speaking Activities – Dave's ESL Café

This site offers dozens of speaking activities teachers from around the world contribute so that other teachers can use them.

http://www.eslcafe.com/idea/index.cgi?Speaking:

The Internet TESL Journal Conversation Questions

Get your students talking with dozens of questions on a number of topics ranging from annoying things to famous people.

http://iteslj.org/questions/

Listening Activities – Dave's ESL Café

This site offers dozens of listening activities teachers from around the world contribute so that other teachers can use them.

http://www.eslcafe.com/idea/index.cgi?Listening

Writing Activities – Dave's ESL Café

This site offers dozens of writing activities teachers from around the world contribute so that other teachers can use them.

http://www.eslcafe.com/idea/index.cgi?Writing

Reading Activities – Dave's ESL Café

This site offers dozens of reading activities teachers from around the world contribute so that other teachers can use them.

http://www.eslcafe.com/idea/index.cgi?Reading

Empower English Tutoring

This is my business' website. There are blog posts for teachers that may be helpful.

http://www.empowerenglishtutoring.com

References

Grand Canyon University ESL

This link is for the vertical sentences activity referenced in the text. There are other great activities on the site as well.

http://gcutesol.weebly.com/you-do-syntax-and-verb-tense.html

Bergquist, C. Emily; Damiani, Mia, Lira-Lane, Cheryl; Long, Katy. "Diversity in an Online Setting: Engaging the English Language Learner." TESOL conference. Toronto. 27 March 2015.

http://gcutesol.weebly.com/you-do-syntax-and-verb-tense.html)

TeachingHistory.org

http://teachinghistory.org/teaching-materials/teaching-guides/21806

Elise Fillpot

Dave's ESL Café by Cliff Pfeil

Rewriting a Story as a Script

http://www.eslcafe.com/idea/index.cgi?display:913574276-18608.txt

Dave's ESL Café by Gareth

Holidays from Hell

http://www.eslcafe.com/idea/index.cgi?display:1175805717-19842.txt

Dave's ESL Café by Paul Careless

Perking Up Pronunciation

http://www.eslcafe.com/idea/index.cgi?display:967454717-16204.txt

Dave's ESL Cafe by Jassica Chang

Smile! Write Poetry with with Similes!

http://www.eslcafe.com/idea/index.cgi?display:1010441111-6686.txt

Dave's ESL Café by Chris

Pass the Story

http://www.eslcafe.com/idea/index.cgi?display:1009080921-4205.txt

Moore, David W., Deborah J. Short, Michael W. Smith, and Alfred W. Tatum. Edge Fundamentals. Student Edition, 1st Ed. ed. Carmel, CA: National Geographic School, 2008. Print.

Made in the USA
Las Vegas, NV
31 January 2022

42718697R00046